BEEN THERE Should've DONE THAT!™

505 Tips for Making the Most of College

Suzette Tyler

Front Porch Press
Haslett, Michigan

BEEN THERE, Should've DONE THAT!™

Copyright © 1997 by Front Porch Press
Written by Suzette Tyler
Cover by b.j. Graphics
Cover photography by Doug Elbinger
Design by Jeff Fillion

Excerpt from Levitz/Noel National Dropout Study, 1991, by permission of USA Group, Noel/Levitz, Iowa City, Iowa. Some quotes have been edited for clarity, brevity, and civility.
Any references to registered trademarks incorporated herein are purely coincidental. These references are not made for the purpose of drawing upon the goodwill and intrinsic value of such trademarks.

Published by Front Porch Press, P.O. Box 234, Haslett, Michigan 48840
Phone: (517) 487-9295. Fax (517) 487-0888. E-mail: styler@voyager.net

ISBN 0-9656086-4-6
Library of Congress Catalog Card Number: 96-62016
Printed in USA

ACKNOWLEDGMENTS

I am immensely grateful to the many young people who shared their thoughts and experiences. It's their voices that give this book meaning. My sincere appreciation also goes to:

- A very dedicated staff in the University Undergraduate Division at Michigan State University.

- Bob Scriver, Jay and Francie Todd for their technical advice and patience.

- Kim Broviac, Karen and Terry Casey, Andrea Funkhouser, Frances Kaneene, Laura Luptowski, Linda Newman, Janet Robison, Kendra Shipps, Lisa Scriver, Diane Wanagat, and Jeff Wolcott for their editing contributions.

- Judy Eyde and Sarah Gilin for their photographic skills.

- Misty Johanson, Aaron Newman, and Lisa Reinhart, my interviewers.

- Pat Sladek, Carol Potter and Gail Dunham for their great encouragement.

- Gary Tyler for his unwavering support despite dirty laundry and an empty refrigerator . . . even *before* the book.

- Adam and Josh Tyler, whose trials and errors inspired me to be a better adviser and mom.

CONTENTS

INTRODUCTION

As an adviser at a major Midwestern university and the parent of two college students whose friends spend much of their summer around the picnic table at our cottage, I've been privy to quite a few conversations reflecting the "should'ves" and "could'ves" of college life. Many of these revelations . . . and in some cases, confessions . . . contain advice that is refreshingly insightful and more encompassing than might be found in an adviser's office. That realization prompted me to gather the thoughts of college students from throughout the United States. Clearly, collegians everywhere encounter similar challenges. With a little editing here and there, their advice is as comprehensive and "expert" as it gets. The following pages will help campus newcomers, as well as veterans, discover how to make the most of their college years—sooner, rather than later. My thanks to all who shared their wisdom.

S. Tyler

"The problem with college is that you figure it out about the time you're ready to graduate."

Senior, Economics, University of Florida

> " I was pretty busy concentrating on my social life during orientation and welcome week. Attending information sessions definitely wasn't a priority. Unfortunately, I missed a few 'key points' that might have made life a little easier . . . like the admissions requirements to the college of business. "

Junior, Communications, Michigan State University

The 'Orientation' Express

To Do's . . . and To Don'ts

Pick an early session. I waited until late in the summer so I could go to orientation with a friend. Forget that! All the courses were closed.

Sophomore, Advertising, University of Florida

Grab a local phone book and take it home. The yellow pages will organize your move by helping find dentists, parking spaces, lofts, whatever . . . .. They'll also help your mom find birthday cakes and other goodies to send to you!

Sophomore, Premed, Cornell University

Don't blow off welcome week programs. Learning about majors and campus activities or how to use the library sounds pretty dull, but it's the ONLY time most of that stuff is offered. It's a quick, painless way to get a lot of information. *GO!*

Senior, Telecommunications, Michigan State University

The summer after high school graduation is a good time to get rid of a college requirement you're dreading—take it at a junior college. I wish I had . . . my math course sucked up so much time during the first semester that I got crummy grades in everything.

Junior, Psychology, Southern Illinois University

Use a map to schedule classes. I didn't . . . and spent a semester running from one end of campus to the other.

Sophomore, Psychology, UCLA

A friend of mine had tons of Advanced Placement credits and ended up taking *all* upper level courses his first semester. He almost flunked out! **AP courses don't always prepare you for college work,** especially the pace. If he had mixed in a couple of beginning level courses or retaken an AP class or two at the college level, his GPA wouldn't have been obliterated.

Sophomore, Advertising, University of Florida

Book Smarts

Buy your books during orientation. If you wait until fall, the lines will be *humongous* and there won't be any used books left to buy.

Junior, Architecture, University of Michigan

Keep your receipts! The text might change or you may decide to drop the class.

Graduate, Biology, Columbia University

Buy books from friends. Sell books to friends. Bookstores rip you off.

Junior, Economics, Duke University

When you buy someone's books, ask for their notes and old tests too.

Senior, Marketing, Ohio University

Placement Tests . . . DON'T GUESS!!!

I must have been psychic when I took the placement tests. I guessed at everything and ended up in classes that were over my head . . . *BIG MISTAKE!!!*

Junior, Environmental Science, Indiana University

Note: If there's a chance you can "place out" of a requirement and placement results are "suggested" rather than mandatory—guess away.

"My plan for decorating our room was awesome—matching comforters, white-eyelet pillows, window valances, and periwinkle blue carpet. My roommate's plan was based on a Pell Grant, the Stafford Loan, and a comforter from home. I quickly ditched the House Beautiful stuff. Our room looks fine, and we get along great."

Sophomore, Nursing, University of Michigan

Dorm Details

You'll Be Glad You Brought . . .

"An electrical outlet extender. There are never enough outlets. Throw in a couple of extension cords, too."

"A _CLEAN_ rug. Old rugs are like death if you have allergies. Don't try to save bucks buying a used rug unless it's _really_ clean."

"A humidifier. In the winter, dorm rooms are the worst. Sore throats and static cling are unending."

"A hide-a-bed. That, or a futon, is great for weekend guests."

"Shower slip-ons. Shower floors are putrid."

"Toilet paper. The college brand is tough on the tush."

The one thing I regret not having at school is a camera. **My entire college career consists of two photos**—and a friend gave me those. There were some great guys and good times that I wish I'd taken pictures of along the way . . . but, then, maybe they'd be incriminating . . . ?!?

Senior, Marketing, Ohio University

You don't have to have your own computer because there are labs all over campus, but it *IS* convenient, especially when it's 1:00 A.M. and there's a foot of snow on the ground.

Junior, Architecture, University of Michigan

A word about computers . . .

Buy your computer through the university. Students get BIG discounts at most schools!

Junior, Packaging, Michigan State University

The good news is having a printer. The *bad* news is everyone knowing you have it. It's like living in a Kinko's annex.

Sophomore, Psychology, UCLA

E-mail makes it a *lot* easier to track down profs. It's also a cheap way to keep in touch with friends at other schools.

Junior, Geology, Arizona State University

You won't get near the computer labs during exam week or when papers are due for a huge lecture course. Start early and beat the rush.

Sophomore, Psychology, UCLA

Housing—Options and Opinions

'Quiet floors' are the way to go. You can always study in your own room and screw around on another floor. *DePaul University*

Freshman dorms *are* loud, but they're good for meeting people and forming study groups since you share a lot of the same classes. *Bowling Green University*

Coed dorms are safer. There are always guys to walk with to and from parties or the library. Plus, guys can build lofts. *Cornell University*

My best friends to this day are the ones I met my freshman year in an all-girl dorm. Girls make better friends when guys aren't around. *Marquette University*

Single rooms are okay for sophomores, but not freshmen. When you're in a single, it's harder to meet people and you don't automatically have someone to walk around campus or go to dinner with. *University of Michigan*

A community john isn't all that bad. There's no waiting when you *need* to use it, no conflict over whose turn it is to clean it and it's a great place to hear what's happening. *DePaul University*

The best room . . . a corner ("larger"), away from the elevator ("too noisy"), on the top floor ("the ceilings are higher for lofts"). *UC-Santa Cruz*

Coed floors are great IF each room has its own bath. If not, I'd request a single-sex floor or wing. *Western Michigan University*

A room by the bathroom sounded convenient until I realized that all the drunks scream and yell there for about 3 hours when they come in at night. *Michigan State University*

You don't mind walking to and from the shower in a towel if you have a Soloflex body . . . but **it's pretty traumatic** if you have bird legs and a body by Budweiser. *Ohio University*

MAKING BIG, small . . .

I'm in a "living/learning" dorm—everyone lives in the same dorm and most of our classes are together. I was worried that it might get old real fast, but it's been great. My friends who aren't in this program spend day after day in huge lectures and never see anyone they know. I know everyone, including the faculty. **It's like a small college with Big Ten sports.**

Sophomore, Lyman Briggs College, Michigan State University

Moving In Musts

"Pay the extra fee to move in a day early. When the cars are lined up and the elevator's jammed, you'll be glad you did."

"Report any room damage *before* you move in so that you won't be charged for it at the end of the year."

"Don't choose the bed by the heat duct. It's always too hot in the winter."

"Don't pound nails in anything without permission."

"Don't be the last one to move in or you'll get the worst bed, desk, dresser, and closet."

The apartment thing . . .

I couldn't wait to live in an apartment, but looking back, it was really more fun in the dorm. I met tons of people and there were more things to do . . . plus, the bathrooms were cleaner.

Graduate, Marketing, University of Wisconsin

Live in the dorm for two years. When you move off campus you never hear about anything, whether it's good parties or good classes.

Senior, Economics, University of Connecticut

Don't move off campus until you have a base of friends. It's isolating.

Senior, Political Science, University of California, Santa Cruz

Once I moved out of the dorm, I was done. It's so easy not to go to class.... **I never ate!** At least the dorm had three squares.... Plus, you need a car. That means gas and insurance!

Sophomore (retired), Engineering, Central Michigan University

Food for thought . . .

If your mom refrains from cooking for about two years before you go to college, you'll love dorm food.

Sophomore, Engineering, Notre Dame

Dorm food gets a bad name. I loved it! Seconds on almost everything, unlimited desserts . . . and no dishes to do.

Graduate, Hospitality Business, Michigan State University

Meal plans *are* cheaper and you'll eat less junk food, *BUT* I wouldn't sign up for more than two meals a day unless you plan on making every breakfast and never eating out. *Riiight!!*

Senior, English, Rutgers

College is a good time to become a vegetarian. *The meat is the worst.*
Sophomore, Advertising, University of Florida

Debit cards are handy if you're not near the dining hall at lunch time. The down side is that it seems like free food so you run through it pretty fast. Cold hard cash instills a little restraint.

Senior, English, Rutgers

There are great restaurants in this town and they all deliver to the dorms. I couldn't figure out where all my money had gone the first semester, until I realized I'd EATEN it! After that, I stuck to my meal plan . . . well, mostly.

Junior, Nursing, University of Michigan

**Face it!
To live with *anyone* 24 hours a day
in a room the size of a closet is
gonna bring on some tense moments,
*friend or not.***

Junior, Sociology, University of Colorado

Roommate Roulette

"Going in Blind" . . . Pros and Cons

I've heard horror stories about "going in blind." If you room with a friend, you know exactly what you're getting. *Indiana University*

I had more problems with the roommates I knew than the ones I didn't. *University of Florida*

I've had four roommates I didn't know. Three were excellent and one was "the roommate from Hell." *University of Rhode Island*

Your best friend may be a slob, but it never bothers you—until you have to live with it. *Ohio University*

I was really pretty shy, so rooming with a friend gave me the confidence to meet more people and try more things. *St. Mary's College*

People aren't as considerate with friends as they are with strangers. It's easy to take advantage of one another and ruin a friendship. *University of Pennsylvania*

My best friend latched onto a guy the first week of school. I might as well have roomed alone! *Michigan State University*

Go for it. If it works out, you've made a friend for life. If it doesn't, it's only temporary. Nothing ventured, nothing gained. *University of Colorado*

I roomed with a high school friend and we ended up barely speaking. I still had to go home to the same town where we both had the same friends . . . her mom knew my mom, her dad was my dad's client . . . **blah, blah, blah**. It wasn't worth it.

Junior, Business, Miami University

Alternatives . . .

My best friend and I requested the same dorm, but not the same room. It was great because we ended up having friends individually and together. If I needed a familiar face or wanted to get out of the room, there was always someplace to go.

Junior, Psychology, Southern Illinois University

Six of us from high school lived together in two rooms. Everyone gravitated to them because it was an 'instant party'. We met a lot of kids that way—but after the first year it was time to move on.

Sophomore, Engineering, University of Michigan

So Bert and Ernie it's not . . .

I was raised with three brothers. My roommate was an only child. We drove each other nuts . . . but I actually missed her over summer break.

Sophomore, English, DePaul

Don't expect too much . . . your roommate won't necessarily be your best friend. That's okay.

Senior, Broadcasting, Marquette University

College is a good time to become the person you want to be. People accept you for who you are now, not who you were **in the third grade.**

Junior, Economics, Williams College

> **It bugs the hell out of you when your roommate's boyfriend is in the room ALL the time, even if he's a nice guy.**
>
> Senior, English, Aquinas College

Before It Gets *Ugly*

My roommate had this "need" to make our room "Party Central" all hours of the day and night. I was too gutless to suggest anything as nerdy as "quiet hours." It lasted until grades came . . .. At least this nerd's still in school.

Junior, Geology, Arizona State University

The kid was *glued* to the Internet . . . that monitor light was *never* off. About three in the morning, I'd want to kill him!

Junior, Biology, University of Michigan

It never frickin' failed. My roommate's boyfriend called the minute my head hit the pillow. In between their arguments, I listened to disgusting mush half the night. I don't know which was worse.

Senior, Education, St. Mary's College

Cutting Through
THE BULL . . .

If something really irritates you—I mean *really*,
say so right from the beginning. If you let it go,
it'll only get worse and end up in a major blowout—
and major bad feelings.

Senior, Education, St. Mary's College

Compromise . . .

Share the air space. Listening to Garth Brooks a thousand times a day can get a *liiittle* irritating if you're into *Pearl Jam.*

Junior, Education, University of Pennsylvania

Take a break. My roommate studied constantly— *in the room!* It was like a monastery. We're all in college to study, but there are times you need to do it elsewhere.

Sophomore, Education, Vanderbilt University

Make a deal. My roommate's a SEGA freak, which totally monopolizes the TV. As long as I get to watch it on Thursday nights, that's OK.

Sophomore, Biology, Kalamazoo College

Borrowing boundaries...

Set limits. After letting my roommate borrow a sweater, my closet became a "free-for-all," especially if I left for the weekend. Make it clear that it's an "ask first" policy and set a specific time that you "need" it returned.

Senior, Psychology, Adelphi University

Clean it. Sharing clothes starts out as a great deal—until the sweater you were planning to wear smells like a gym bag or a brewery.

Senior, Business, Northern Illinois University

Know when to throw in the towel . . .

Don't drag it out. My first clue should have been the day I arrived and found the entire room rearranged and *my* desk in the hall! It was downhill from there. If it's bad to start with, it'll only get worse. There are usually a few "no show" spaces available in the fall. Request one.

Junior, Psychology, Southern Illinois University

Gut it out. It's just where you sleep. Spend time in other rooms and chalk the semester up as "an experience." It'll give you time to find a roommate you *do* like for the next semester.

Senior, Human Development, University of Connecticut

TOP 10

Ways To Make Your Roommate Happy

10 Buy your own shampoo and deodorant—*and* use it.

9 Wash your cereal bowl and socks *before* they're green and fuzzy.

8 Keep your wet towel off the beds

7 Keep visits from high school friends down to something less than a week.

6 Don't hit the "snooze" a thousand times for an eight o'clock you're not going to anyway.

5 Keep your beverages off the computer.

4 Don't erase the answering machine and then announce, "Someone called but I don't remember who . . . ." Write it down.

3 Remember, it's a *dorm* room, not a romantic hideaway.

2 Don't disappear when it's time to pay for the pizza . . . or anything else.

1 **Flush.**

"I cried every day for the first month. I couldn't even call home because I couldn't talk without sobbing. You just want to sit and do nothing . . . and that's the worst thing you can do. Force yourself to get busy."

Junior, Psychology, Southern Illinois University

Bummers

"I went to preschool with the same kids I graduated from high school with. I *never* had a moment of trying to figure out where I fit in—*until college!*"

Sophomore, Economics, Williams College

The hardest thing to get used to is doing things alone. In high school I never even went to the bathroom alone much less *ate* alone. You have to learn to walk up to people and start talking.

Junior, Chemical Engineering, M.I.T.

Don't go home the first month. It only makes it harder when you come back. Besides, that's when everyone is anxious to make friends and there's a lot going on.

Junior, Engineering, Notre Dame

Write to all your friends when you first get there. You'll have mail for weeks!

Junior, Chemical Engineering, M.I.T.

The best way to get over being homesick is not to go home.

Senior, Political Science, University of California, Santa Cruz

Long distance relationships are tough to pull off. The biggest mistake I made was having a girlfriend at another school the first two years. Neither of us really *enjoyed* college. It makes you older than you are.

Senior, English, Denison University

It was hard to go back after Christmas break my freshman year. I was still wondering whether I'd picked the right college. I'm glad I did. Any college is fine once you find your group of friends.

Sophomore, Economics, Williams College

GimmeSpace...

There's no privacy in the dorms. The first year was like not being able to breathe. I eventually found a family off campus who needed a baby-sitter and it was like reconnecting with **the real world . . . kids, pets, houses.** They've become my family away from home. It's really a nice break from the dorm.

Sophomore, Physical Therapy, Northwestern College

The Ex-Jock Syndrome. Guys that were real jocks in high school tend to gain a lot of weight if they don't play anything in college—especially with "all-you-can-eat" food lines. You have to make a point of working out or getting involved in intramurals.

Junior, Psychology, Southern Illinois University

Fat and broke. Everyone gets the late night 'munchies', especially if you eat dinner at five o'clock. Stock up on your own supply of good-ies—fat free, of course. It's healthier and cheaper than hitting the vending machines or ordering take-out . . . as long as you don't polish everything off in the first hour.

Sophomore, Economics, Williams College

The 'Freshman 15' isn't from dorm food. It's alcohol and ordering pizza when you're trashed at 3:00 A.M.

Junior, Business, Miami of Ohio

"I see kids get so hung up on grades that they miss everything else. College is more than a GPA."

Junior, Chemical Engineering, MIT

Note: 37% of students who drop out have GPAs of 2.5 or above. For reasons other than academics, they have not "connected" in the college setting. (Levitz & Noel National Dropout Study)

Carpe Diem, Definitely!

Seize the day! ("Deul Poet's Society")

There's a lot of cool stuff on campus, but you have to look for it. I was so caught up in making friends and writing papers, that college was no bigger than my dorm. It took me a while but I finally got involved in a campus group, and through that, a research project. I should have done it sooner.

Senior, Physiology, Michigan State University

If I had it to do over I'd go to more than just football games and parties. There were excellent speakers, concerts, theater . . ..

Graduate, Marketing, University of Wisconsin

All anyone wanted to talk about during job interviews was what I'd done *outside* of the classroom . . ..

Graduate, Engineering, University of Michigan

READ everything!

Bulletin boards, the campus newspaper, mail—I didn't pay much attention to any of it and I missed a whole lot of things because I didn't . . .. **I could have been scuba diving** in San Salvador for my natural science requirement!

Graduate, Humanities, Michigan State University

Join . . .

Definitely join a club affiliated with your major. That's where you'll meet faculty and make contacts with people in your field.

Senior, Accounting, Indiana University

Sign up for dorm rep, floor rep, whatever . . . or volunteer for a committee. You'll meet tons of people and find out everything happening on campus.

Sophomore, Communications, John Carroll University

I thought all the activities and clubs on campus were stupid because they didn't really do anything. Now that I'm in a career, I realize **THAT was what THIS is all about.**

Graduate, Economics, Carleton College

GO GLOBAL!!!

I'd sell my car, my stereo, and everything I own to repeat the experience I had in an overseas study program! I learned more during that semester than all the rest put together.

Senior, English, Denison University

*Note: If a foreign study program is not available through your college, contact:
College Consortium for International Studies (800) 453-6956.*

> People are the best part. Having friends makes college easier.
>
> *Sophomore, Education, Vanderbilt University*

Go to dorm "icebreakers" and floor activities. Some can be a little nerdy, but they're good for laughs. You'll meet a lot of others who don't want to spell their name with their hips either....

Sophomore, Engineering, University of Michigan

Long lines are a pain but they're great for meeting people. I make a point of talking to everyone, everywhere. You find out a lot of good stuff.

Senior, Psychology, Grand Valley State University

Be a sport.

Even if you're not a jock, participate in sports—intramural, coed, whatever. It's a great way to meet people.

Sophomore, Speech Pathology, Butler University

Don't overlook the obscure varsity or club sports . . . the perks are the same whether it's football or fencing. I've made great friends, traveled, *and* I get to register early!

Junior, Michigan State University

I've gotten to know upperclassmen because of playing a sport. They not only tell you "what's up" but will give you a ride there.

Sophomore, Premed, Cornell University

"Choosing courses can make or break you in college. The better you are at it, the better your grades and the less your aggravation."

Junior, Sociology, University of Colorado

Choosing Courses

In the beginning . . .

Even if you're Einstein, the first semester is a big adjustment. Don't get so hung up on getting out in four years that you bite off more than you can chew. You can always pick up extra credits somewhere along the line.

Junior, Labor Studies, Saint Joseph's University

Trust me, freshmen "orientation" courses are *totally worthwhile*. I had a far better handle on **what to do and where to find it** than my friends who *didn't* take the course. It eliminates a lot of trial and error.

Junior, Education, Western Michigan University

I was valedictorian in high school, so it was pretty discouraging when I had to work a whole lot harder— **for C's!** I should have started with an easier load and built up some confidence.

Sophomore, Premed, Cornell University

Balance Is Everything!

It's better to take fewer credits and do *well* than just *get by* with more. GPAs are too hard to bring up!

Junior, Human Development, University of Connecticut

The number of *courses* you take is more important than the number of *credits.* Four courses worth 16 credits are more manageable than five courses worth 15 credits.

Junior, Kinesiology, University of Michigan

Don't schedule too many heavy reading courses in the same semester, and *definitely* not more than one lab!

Sophomore, Premed, Cornell University

Voices of Experience . . .

"Continue a language immediately. If you wait until the second semester, everyone else will be coming off the first . . . very fluently."

"Don't take 300 and 400 level courses as a freshman. The competition will kill you."

"Don't let the title or course description fool you. Some of the worst classes *sound* fascinating."

"Be choosy. If a class or prof doesn't seem 'right,' change sections or drop it immediately while you can still get another class."

"Take electives. They'll help you decide on a major and make college more fun."

Smart students know exactly which courses and instructors to take and which to avoid. I guess that's what makes them smart.

Junior, Geology, Arizona State University

If you need an easy course or professor, ask an athlete.

Senior, Education, University of Tennessee

Note: Because of the enormous time commitment during their season of competition, athletes must be very careful to balance their schedules and aware of which classes can help them do that.

F R O M   T H E   A D V I S O R

F R O M   T H E   A D V I S O R

Know What You're Getting . . .

Talk to upperclassmen. Students often know better than advisers what courses and profs are best.

Check the bookstore for a book that rates the instructors.

Sit in on a class the term before or stand outside the classroom and talk to students as they come out.

Beware of empty seats. If the only section that's still open has lots of seats available and it's not an eight-o'clock, chances are there's a reason.

Read the syllabus. Borrow it or browse through it at the bookstore.

GOODAdvice

If I'd talked to an adviser instead of just my friends **I could have saved about $5,000** and a lot of grief. Between the classes I took that I didn't need and the semester I added by missing the application date to my major, a few visits to the advising office would have really paid off.

Senior, Nursing, Michigan State University

Don't believe everything you read. I spent the summer taking a course I absolutely hated only to find out that the requirement had been dropped! You need to talk with advisers on a regular basis. The printed requirements for majors aren't always up to date, or they'll accept something other than what's listed.

Graduate, Michigan State University

You can mess up your entire program *and* graduation date if you miss a course that isn't offered every semester, especially if it's a prerequisite for other courses you need! Have an adviser review your four-year course plan periodically.

Junior, Chemical Engineering, M.I.T.

"Pick the professor, *not* the time of day."

Graduate, Economics, University of Wisconsin

The Perfect Schedule

I used to pore over the schedule book for hours trying to arrange the perfect schedule. **No way would I consider a class before 10:00 or after 2:00**, and definitely no Friday afternoons. I *never even looked* to see *who* was teaching the course. After getting 'hosed' on instructors a few times it finally occurred to me that my method might be flawed . . . .

Senior, Economics, University of Connecticut

A good professor can make the most boring course on campus fascinating . . . and vice-versa.

Senior, Economics, Carleton College

Nothing grinds you more than a friend having the same class with another instructor who's a lot more interesting . . . *and* less work. **You'll kick yourself for the whole term.**

Junior, Economics, Duke University

Know thyself . . .

I like eight o'clocks. I roll out of bed, throw on a sweatshirt and go. Then I can study in the afternoon when it's quieter, and have my evenings free.

Sophomore, Communications, John Carroll University

Eight o'clocks are the worst! Nobody goes to bed before 2 A.M. Ultimately, you end up sleep deprived and cutting class. Guaranteed.

Junior, Advertising, University of Florida

Register for an extra class.
After the first week or so, drop the course you like the least.
Sophomore, Psychology, UCLA

The three-hour classes, one night a week are great! It's one night not wasted screwing around in the dorm, and the prof always lets you go early.
Senior, Marketing, Ohio University

Schedule classes back to back.
You're less likely to cut.
Junior, Business, University of Alabama

Summer is a good time to take difficult courses. Instructors are more relaxed, classes are smaller, and the competition is less. It's perfect for taking labs.
Junior, Engineering, Notre Dame

It's now or never . . .

Man, there are *so many* courses I wish I'd taken in college. I always kind of thought I'd like broadcasting . . . so how is it I never even took a course in it? What a waste.

Graduate, Marketing, Ohio University

Don't waste money on blowoff courses. Take what you're really interested in.

Junior, Engineering, Notre Dame

Don't take "no" for an answer . . .

If a class will fill before my enrollment date, I find someone with an earlier enrollment and have them "hold" it for me. It takes a coordinated effort, but it's worth it.

Junior, Packaging, Michigan State University

It was closed but I went to the class every day, waiting for someone to drop. No one ever did, but the prof eventually took pity on me and let me in anyway.

Sophomore, Psychology, UCLA

If you can't get into a class, talk directly to the instructor. Say something to set yourself apart from the *other* 20 people who are trying to add it—mention a colleague who "suggested the class," talk about your "special interest" in his area . . . whatever it takes.

Senior, Marketing, Ohio University

> **"You are basically *screwed* if you miss a math class!"**
>
> Sophomore, Economics, Williams College

m..mm..mmm...MATH!

Famous Last Words

"Nobody collected the homework so I figured I'd just wait and do it later . . .."

"I didn't want to waste money taking the math I placed into, since I'd already had it in high school . . .."

"I couldn't understand the instructor so I decided to teach myself out of the book instead of wasting time in class . . .."

"Math was easy for me in high school and the first chapters covered stuff I knew, so I didn't actually *work* the problems . . .."

"It was just a bad day when I took the placement test so I enrolled in the next level . . .."

CALCULUS kills...

Even if you place into it, think twice before starting with calculus *unless* you've had it in high school. Most of the class has, and you'll be at a definite disadvantage if you haven't.

Junior, Economics, Duke University

Note: If that is the only math required by your major and a stellar grade isn't necessary, try it.

Solutions . . .

"Take math at a junior college. Classes are smaller."

"Don't buy a calculator without a backup battery."

"Do practice problems without looking at the answers first."

"Look for small classes. The seating capacity of each classroom is usually in the schedule book."

"You can't cram for math tests. It doesn't work. Keep up with the daily stuff so you won't have to."

"Math opens the door to some great majors. Hang in there."

T.A. tips . . .

Find a good one. Most math classes have a common final so it's important to get a good T.A.—*preferably one who helps write the final.* Ask around. If the department won't tell you which section a T.A. you want is teaching, call him and ask.

Sophomore, Engineering, University of Michigan

Change sections. If you can't understand a T.A., switch sections right away. But don't assume he's a bad teacher just because he has an accent.

Junior, Engineering, M.I.T.

Having a T.A. is like dating—find out what you have in common and then make the most of it. *University of Tennessee*

Regroup . . .

DO NOT, for *any* reason, go on to the next math level if you barely got through the first one. You'll get killed. Repeat the course.

Sophomore, Engineering, Central Michigan University

If you're lost after the first few weeks, drop back to a lower math. I **was beating my brains out** in calculus and barely getting a C. I dropped back to precalculus, got an A, and ended up getting an A+ the next semester in the same course that had been killing me before. I probably would have dropped out of engineering if I hadn't been able to fill the gap between high school and college math. It's a big jump.

Sophomore, Engineering, University of Michigan

The 'NEVER FAIL' Formula

Before, **not after.** Doing assignments *before* lectures instead of *after* is the secret to math. I know exactly where I'm having trouble and what I need to learn.
Miami University

Now, **not then.** Don't wait until you're totally lost to get help. See the instructor or get a tutor right away.
Western Michigan University

All, **not some.** You have to be a maniac about math homework. Do *all* the problems.
Arizona State University

Sooner, **not later.** No matter how well I understood things in class, if I waited a couple days to do the homework, I was lost. Do homework ASAP.
Albion College

> "I was an expert at avoiding courses that required writing and at finding papers I could "borrow." Unfortunately, that made for some tense moments when I discovered how much writing was expected in my first real job. It would definitely have been smarter to have perfected that skill in college."

Graduate, Marketing, University of Wisconsin

The 'Write' Stuff

Foolproof fundamentals . . .

Confirm your thesis. I put *hours* into a huge paper only to find out that I'd done it wrong! DON'T write a word until the professor has approved your thesis.

Junior, Business, University of Michigan

Start early and keep revising. Set up a timetable for the outline, research, and rough draft. Then *stick to it!*

Senior, English, Aquinas College

Submit a rough draft. *ALWAYS* ask the T.A. or the professor to review your rough draft before turning in the final paper. They're more likely to grade a paper favorably if they've "helped" write it.

Sophomore, Art, Bowling Green University

QUICK TIPS

"Use quotes from the lecture."

"Pick a topic in which the professor isn't an expert."

"Pick a topic that can be used for more than one course."

"Proofread out loud."

"Don't plagiarize it. Cite it."

"I'd like to go back to my freshman year . . .
get some good grades . . .
make more intelligent decisions . . .
I just didn't have a clue."

Senior, Economics, University of Florida

Get a Clue

CLUE #1 Self-Discipline!

The trick is to sit down and study when there are
more interesting possibilities available . . . and there
always are!

Sophomore, Speech Pathology, Butler University

There's always someone who wants to do *something*. All I had to hear was, "Wanna hoop?" and I was gone. After grades came, I left my Nikes at home.

University of Toledo

Cable's a killer. I'd always tell myself, "I'll just watch *a few* minutes of the movie . . .." Two hours later, there I sat.

University of Tennessee

SEGA® sucked up my entire freshman year.

Albion College

Dorm rooms are a setup for failure. You're surrounded by every distraction you can possibly think of. *Junior, Geology, Arizona State University*

Don't hang around people who do nothing but party—unless you plan a career in the family business or the local car wash.

Graduate, Marketing, University of Wisconsin

This year, unlike last, I room with guys who get good grades. It rubs off.

Junior, Education, Central Michigan University

The first few weeks are great! You're meeting people, partying, no tests, no papers . . . Then, *wham*!! You've got everything due in the same week. If you weren't hitting the books right along, you'll spend the rest of the term digging yourself out!

Senior, Political Science, University of California, Santa Cruz

My brother, who's not in college, works 40 or 50 hours a week at his job. When I'm sick of studying I try to ask myself if I've put in that many hours. It's **definitely a reality check.** You need to think of school as your job.

Junior, Engineering, Notre Dame

"Where else is 15 hours a week considered a 'Full Load'?"

T-shirt worn by Michigan State University Student

RX: For good grades . . . PAARRTY!!!

College was *the* best time . . . I never missed a party *AND* I got great grades! The trick is to get up each morning and plan exactly what you want to do that night—party or whatever. Then tell yourself you can't go until you're done studying. It's like a reward. If I thought nothing was going on I'd waste the whole day and end up falling asleep in front of the TV at night.

Graduate, English, Ohio University

CLUE #2 Time Management!

I can't even say I'm on probation because of partying. I just became **a big couch potato.** For the first time in my life there wasn't anyone to tell me what to do or when to do it, so I didn't do anything—including study.

Freshman, Engineering, Michigan State University

TIME...

Study between classes. I spent a lot of time watching TV during the day until I figured out that if I *studied*, I could have my nights free. Don't go back to the dorm between classes. Find someplace to study. *John Carroll University*

Stay out of bed. *Any* time I didn't have classes, I slept. It's a *bad* habit to get into. *Rollins College*

Prioritize. I got so involved with club activities in my major that my grades were barely high enough to *get into* the major. *Michigan State University*

...Use it or lose it!

Make a calendar for the entire semester. I combine the dates from all the course syllabi onto *one* calendar and hang it where I can see it *daily*. It's a visual thing. You have to *see* it. *University of Wisconsin*

Set specific 'study hours.' For me, the toughest part of studying is getting started. I set aside a specific time for every day. It's like going to a job; you *have* to be there. *Cornell University*

Make lists. In high school you can do it when it comes to mind or when someone reminds you. In college there's too much to remember and *nobody's* going to remind you! *Adelphi University*

If you do nothing else in college, at least *go to class!*

Junior, Business, Miami University

Just *Go!*

Even if I'd partied all night, I dragged my body to class. Other people's notes don't work . . . *you have to hear it yourself.*

Graduate, English, Indiana University

Sitting in a classroom is the easiest part of college and it cuts study time in half. Why make it hard on yourself—*go!*

Senior, Journalism, University of Iowa

Instructors take it personally if you cut a lot. Not having an attendance *requirement* doesn't mean they won't take it out on your grade.

Junior, Education, Central Michigan University

I used to think the first couple of classes were a waste because everyone's still dropping and adding. **Wrong!** That's when the instructor announces changes in the syllabus and when you should decide whether to drop the class. *Junior, Business, University of Alabama*

Talk about horror stories . . . I had one of those classes where you decide you'll learn more by reading the book than by going to class. I cut quite a few, including the one when a change in the final exam date was announced.

Senior, Communications, University of Toledo

> "It's not how smart you are—everyone is.
> It's whether you know how to study.
> I see really bright guys that get "nothing"
> grades and average guys that get 4-points.

Senior, Economics, University of Florida

Grinding It Out

Teachers are in your face every day in high school, so it's easy to stay on track and keep up the pace. It doesn't work that way in college. You set your own pace. If you don't study, it's your problem . . ..

Sophmore, Advertising, University of Florida

My roommate *never* studied and got great grades. It took me a while to face the fact that *I* couldn't do that. While he kicked back and had a good old time, I dragged myself to the library. It was frustrating, but that's life. You have to do what works best *for you*.

Senior, Communications, University of Toledo

Don't Get BEHIND!!!

The biggest difference between high school and college is the *amount of reading*. It's **impossible to catch up** if you get behind.

Sophomore, Biology, Kalamazoo College

ESP helps. I try to predict test questions when I'm studying or sitting in a lecture. It forces me to focus on what's important.

Sophomore, History, University of Pennsylvania

Know what you need to know. I wasted a lot of time reading and not learning what I needed to. I eventually figured out that if I look at the chapter-end review questions and all the chapter headings, they pretty much tell you exactly what you're supposed to learn.

Junior, Criminal Justice, Saint Joseph's University

Read ahead of the lecture. It was *incredible* how much easier Chemistry was when I began reading the assignments BEFORE the lecture. It was like a different course.

Sophomore, Engineering, University of Michigan

Highlighters are overrated. I can end up with the whole book in yellow and still not understand a thing. Taking notes and putting everything in my own words works better . . . and it's easier to stay awake.

Senior, Education, St. Mary's College

Where to do it . . . (study!)

Get out of the room! You'll end up talking on the phone, watching TV, cleaning out drawers—just about anything to avoid studying!

Graduate, Economics, Rollins College

Studying in bed is an illusion. After 15 minutes, you're zonked.

Junior, Anthropology, Macalester College

If your door's open, people wander in and you find yourself listening to a lot of B.S. you could have lived without.

Junior, Engineering, Notre Dame

The department libraries are perfect for studying because no one uses them except the brains.

Junior, Political Science, Ohio State University

I know too many people at the library so **I study for tests at Krogers.** It's perfect . . . quiet, soft music, and when I need a break I cruise the aisles and pick up samples.

Senior, Marketing, Ohio University

Study Groups . . .

They're good for clarifying what you need to study alone.

Sophomore, Education, Vanderbilt University

There's always someone who likes to impress everyone with how much he knows. Include him in your group.

Senior, Business, University of Toledo

I don't believe in study groups. The logistics are difficult and they waste time. The buddy system works *much* better. A friend and I had almost every class together. Before tests or writing papers, we always bounced things off one another. Between the two of us, there wasn't much we missed.

Senior, Marketing, Ohio University

Cramming quickies . . .

Memorize the chapter summaries and definitions. It's too late to learn it all, so don't even try.

Senior, Psychology, Grand Valley State University

You'll be better at 'B.S.'ing your way through a test if you get some sleep. All-nighters aren't worth it.

Junior, Political Science, Ohio State University

There are times that cramming is unavoidable and covering a few weeks of backlog is attainable. But the whole semester . . . naaahh.

Junior, Sociology, University of Colorado

"You have to learn how to get the most out of boring instructors and classes that are 'cattle calls.' It's a trick to remain conscious, let alone learn something.

Junior, Geology, Arizona State University

Classroom Cues

I sit front and center. I can tell you what every person in class is wearing and not much of anything else when I sit in the back.

Sophomore, Art, Bowling Green University

Profs watch the faces up front. I like to sit there since I'm a slow writer and I can catch the instructor's eye when he's going too fast.

Junior, Business, Miami of Ohio

Always **get the phone number** of at least one person in every class. At midnight, when you can't read your notes or can't remember what chapters are on the test, you can find out.

Senior, Education, University of Tennessee

Shy, but sly . . .

There were office hours after class every day, but nobody ever used them except me. It was like private tutoring. Even if the instructor can't talk with you right after class, it's a good time to schedule an appointment for when he can.

Graduate, Management, Ferris State University

There were only sixty-three kids in my entire high school class—**no way was I gonna raise my hand in a lecture with 300!** Eventually I started keeping a list of my questions and talking with the professor during his office hours . . . or I used e-mail.

Sophomore, Advertising, University of Florida

Make the most of lousy profs . . .

I keep the syllabus or course outline in the front of my notebook so that I can figure out what the point of the lecture is. You can't always tell.

Junior, Psychology, Southern Illinois University

I hated his class. The lectures were deadly. I finally forced myself to drop by during office hours. Somehow, after discussing a few points and getting to know him, his lectures seemed more interesting. At least, I could stay awake . . . .

Junior, Education, Central Michigan University

Big tips for small classes . . .

Don't be late or leave early. It really ticks profs off. Besides that's when they usually make announcements or get to the point.

Sophomore, English, DePaul University

Volunteer to answer questions you *do* know so you won't be called on for the ones you don't.

Junior, Psychology, Colgate University

Look fascinated. Even if you're bored out of your mind, don't touch that newspaper!

Sophomore, Anthropology, Macalester College

"I'd think to myself "I don't need to write that down, I'll remember it." A few days later, it was like "*what* did he say . . .?"**"

Junior, Economics, Duke University

Note: Scientifically speaking, you lose 70% of information within 24 hours.

Notes on Notetaking

School's never been easy for me so tape recording my classes helped *a lot*. I still took notes, but I could *relax and listen better* to what was being said because I always knew that I could "fast forward" to anything I needed to hear again.

Graduate, Management, Ferris State University

Not everything a prof says is important. But if you haven't read the assignments *before* the lecture you'll end up writing down every word anyway because you don't know what is and what isn't.

Junior, Biology, University of Michigan

Note: Get the instructor's permission to record the lecture.

Listen . . . Think . . .
SUMMARIZE!!!

I had tons of notes—I copied *every word* the professor said. Actually, I was so busy writing that **I didn't understand a thing . . ..**

Junior, Criminal Justice, Saint Joseph's University

Watch the eyes. If the instructor looks down at his notes before speaking, the next sentence is probably important.

Senior, English, Rutgers University

Note-taking services are the best thing going. Use them to fill in the gaps—*not* in place of going to class!

Junior, Geology, Arizona State University

Pay attention to when you're not paying attention. It's impossible to keep your mind from wandering. Know when you're doing it and mark the spot in your notes so you can get the information later.

Junior, Business, Marquette University

Listen for...
KEY PHRASES

"to sum it up . . ."

"remember that . . ."

"in other words . . ."

"in my opinion . . ."

"the turning point . . ."

"notice that . . ."

"point #1, #2, etc."

"the basic reason . . ."

"a prime example . . ."

"in conclusion . . ."

I lost a notebook with *six weeks* of notes in it! Your name, phone, course, and section number should be on *every* book you own.

Junior, Political Science, Ohio State University

Instead of doing nothing between classes, I clean up my notes. If I don't re-read and clarify them sometime the same day, they never make sense later.

Junior, Labor Studies, Saint Joseph's University

Tricks of the trade . . .

Be creative. I use a four-color pen, draw pictures, whatever it takes to make notes memorable.

Speak up. Don't be afraid to ask an instructor to slow down if he's going too fast.

Date your notes. It's easier to refer to your notes or compare them with others if they're dated.

One's good. Two's better. If I miss a class, I get notes from two different people. It's easier to pinpoint which information is really important.

In high school there were *zillions* of tests, quizzes, reports, extra credit . . . you name it. In college, it might be just a midterm and a final. If you mess up on one, your grade's shot!

Senior, Education, University of Tennessee

Test Tips

1 Talk with the instructor before tests.

The odds are against you on first tests because you have no idea what to expect. I make a point of seeing the prof a few days before, just to make sure I'm "focusing on the right material." In other words, I want HOT TIPS. Taking a couple of "confused" classmates along makes him even more cooperative. Don't waste your time with TA's unless they know what's on the test. Some do, some don't.

Senior, Marketing, Ohio University

Find old exams.

Hustling old tests is worth the effort. Profs seldom change them much. Even if they do, an old test will tell you which concepts you're expected to know and how well to know them. Check with students who have taken the course, the department, fraternity test files, the library, or the professor himself.

Senior, Management Information Systems, Ohio University

3 You gotta *UNDERSTAND.*

High school is memorization and regurgitation. Here you have to think. I remember bombing the first test after studying my brains out. Some of that stuff I swore I'd never seen before. It's called "applying the principle." You have to *understand the concept* well enough to see how it relates to something you've never discussed in class. That's where most kids get killed.

Junior, Engineering, Notre Dame

4 Know the vocabulary of the course.

T.A.s are looking for key words and phrases, and not much else when there's 200 to 300 essay tests to correct. The more you use, the better your grade. Actually, if you don't understand the terminology well, you'll have trouble with multiple choice and true/false tests too.

Graduate, Marketing, University of Wisconsin

5 Make the most of quizzes.

Quizzes are an easy way to boost your grade because they cover fewer chapters. It's your chance to make up for what you're going to screw up on the final.

Senior, Marketing, Ohio University

6 Scantrons error.

Computerized test-scoring isn't perfect. Smudges can kill you. If your grade seems incorrect, ask to see the answer sheet. It meant a full grade for me . . ..

Graduate, Physiology, Michigan State University

7 Learn from your mistakes.

Some profs only post the test scores and never return the actual test. It's a pain, but ask to review the corrected test in his office so you know exactly what you missed. Otherwise, you'll repeat the same mistakes the next time.

Sophomore, No Preference, Michigan State University

66

**Kids know what it takes to get an A.
I think, consciously or unconsciously,
most decide they don't want to work
that hard.**

99

Junior, Honors College, Michigan State University

The ABC's of GPA's

Grade grubbing . . .

Grade errors happen, but most kids just figure they didn't do well on the exam and don't bother to check, especially if it's during the summer. The 2.0 I got in a class was supposed to have been a 2.5—not a big difference, but enough to get me off probation.

Junior, Communications, Michigan State University

***Always* go over a test after it's graded** to make sure there aren't any errors and to see if you can "milk" it for a few more points. Just don't overdo it. Profs get ticked.

Senior, Psychology, Adelphi University

Ask the T.A. to reread a paper if you think it deserves a better grade. I've never *not* been given the extra points.

Senior, H.R.I., Michigan State University

Ask for extra credit or to rewrite a test or paper you've bombed. Some profs won't let you, but most will.

Senior, Accounting, Indiana University

Don't question an instructor's grading in front of other students. He'll be reluctant to help you.

Senior, English, Denison University

When "easy" doesn't do it . . .

Tough courses psyche me up. I'm more disciplined because I know I have to be, so my grades are better.

Senior, Accounting, Valparaiso University

The trouble with **"gut" courses** is that instead of using them as an opportunity to grab a good grade, you just blow them off and end up getting a C . . . or worse. They really ARE easy if you GO to class and DO the work.

Sophomore, Economics, Williams College

An Incomplete can save you from disaster if doing the remaining assignments or preparing for the exam is beyond hope. Ask the prof for an "I". It's worth a shot.

Junior, Psychology, Southern Illinois University

Make-up tests are 100 percent harder!

Junior, Human Development, University of Connecticut

The Pass/Fail option is a good way to take courses you're weak in without destroying your GPA. But make sure which majors will or won't accept them.

Junior, Biology, University of Michigan

DROP It!!!

It's not a sin to drop a class . . . it's good course management. **Don't take the hit** of a poor grade. It's discouraging and can ruin a GPA.

Sophomore, Premed, Cornell University

Note: Make sure you know the final date for dropping a class, with and without a refund, and whether it will affect your financial aid.

Help, I've fallen...
REPEAT RULES

Repeat an "F" as soon as possible. It's the quickest way to raise a GPA.

Don't bother repeating a 1.0 or a 1.5 unless you know you can do considerably better than a 2.0—or a higher grade is *required*.

DO repeat a low grade if the course is a "building block" for a series of courses you'll need . . . *especially MATH!*

Repeat courses at a junior college. The transfer repeat usually wipes out the original grade—at a cheaper price.

Note: Repeat rules vary among colleges. Check with your adviser.

"An average student can get the same results as a smart one if he plays his cards right.

Senior, English, Denison University

Gaining the Edge

It's weird, you're the one who's only eighteen years old, but it's up to you to make the effort to talk with Ph.D.s if you want them to get to know you. I always try to find out what they're into, what research they're doing. If it's monkeys . . . I ask about monkeys.

Junior, Michigan State University

I got an A+ in one class and a D+ in another on *the exact same paper!* The A+ was from a T.A. I'd talked with a lot, and the D+ from one I hadn't.

Junior, Environmental Science, University of Michigan

Don't underestimate the power of kissing butt!

Junior, Sociology, University of Colorado

THINK
THINK
THINK About It . . .

Your grade on everything you write . . . tests, term papers,
whatever . . . gets down to one opinion—the instructor's.
If he likes you and thinks you're putting in effort, it can
be **the difference between an A and a C.**

Junior, Business, Miami University

Attitude is everything . . .

Instructors will bend over backwards to help kids who are really trying. Make every effort to let them know you are.

Junior, Journalism, University of Iowa

If you go in thinking "this sucks, the prof's a dork," you'll hate the course. Just sit there and figure you're gonna make the most of it. I aced a really nasty course that way. I stopped by the prof's office once a week just to talk. He loved me. Too bad I didn't figure that out in high school.

Sophomore, Lansing Community College

Write thank-you notes to guest speakers and file their names in your Rolodex. You never know when one of them might be able to help you with a summer job or internship.

Senior, English, Aquinas College

MENTOR magic . . .

A friend of mine worked on a project with one of our professors. That relationship eventually allowed him to accompany the prof to Poland and to present research to several economic groups. He was later **recommended for Phi Beta Kappa** by the professor and ultimately accepted at a prestigious law school. I could have been the one volunteering for that project . . ..

Senior, Economics, Hope College

It's who you know . . .

I wasn't exactly the best student, by a long shot, but I had established a good relationship with an instructor in my major, and he recommended me for the internship. Voila! Six months in the Virgin Islands!

Senior, Hospitality Management, Michigan State University

. . . and who you don't.

Grad school applications ask for three *personal* recommendations from undergraduate faculty. I barely remembered any of their *names!* I know they didn't remember mine!!!

Graduate, Telecommunications, Michigan State University

My biggest regret when I look back at college is not having used the office hours.

Graduate, Physiology, Michigan State University

Learn who the professors are. If one of them is an expert in a field you're interested in or he's from a grad school you're thinking about, then he's the one you want to get to know and his recommendation is the one you want to have.

Graduate, Biology, Columbia University

You can cut study time in half just by chatting with instructors during office hours. They'll pinpoint what is and what isn't important in the lectures and readings. Most are glad to talk with you since they have to be there anyway.

Senior, Education, University of Tennessee

Before asking a prof for help, read the assignments. It's obvious if you haven't, and she'll resent you wasting her time.

Senior, Political Science, Western Michigan University

> "I sat back thinking that the right major would just pop into my head. It didn't. By the end of my sophomore year I still didn't have a clue."

Senior, Economics, University of Connecticut

The MAJOR Dilemma

Don't just sit there . . .

I probably spent more time checking out used cars than checking out majors. I worried about it a lot but I never got off my butt and did anything to find out what each major was really about. When the time came that I had to decide, I didn't have much more information than I did as a freshman—it was kind of like throwing a dart.

Senior, Economics, University of Connecticut

Declare a major even if you're unsure. You can always change it, but in the meantime you'll be on mailing lists and hear about special programs and activities that you otherwise would know nothing about. College becomes a whole different experience—*and your adviser will know your name!*

Senior, Management Information Systems, Ohio University

ADVISOR

F R O M   T H E   A D V I S O R

Strategies for Making a Choice...

Talk to professors in courses you enjoy about what majors and careers are related to that field.

Know what's available. In addition to the majors, get a list of minors, cognates, specializations, or whatever. They add focus to a degree and make you more marketable.

Write to graduate schools and go to their on-campus presentations. You'll get an idea of what's out there and what you need to do as an undergraduate to prepare for it.

Use the career center. Counselors, testing, and career files are all there to help you.

Talk to people in the career you think you'd like about what's going on in that field and how to get there. Ask to job shadow.

Due to a lot of screw-ups my freshman year, my major isn't exactly what I'd like it to be. Unfortunately, by the time I decided what that was, I'd already taken—and bombed—some of the required courses. It's like if you're even thinking about a major, find out the requirements!

Senior, Economics, University of Florida

Biology was always my thing so that's what I majored in. At the time, I didn't realize there were lots of other majors related to that field that could have opened up totally different career options. . .

Senior, Biology, Michigan State University

"I love [fill in the blank] but I don't know how I'd make a career of it."
(Music, cars, nature, computers—or whatever your interest.)

IMAGINE

How could I be paid to:

Write about it?

Talk about it?

Perform it?

Assist people who do it?

Create a product related to it?

Sell a product related to it?

Provide a service to people interested in it?

Learn about it?

Note: Adapted from Patrick Combs' Major in Success (Ten Speed Press, 1994), a terrific book for helping students connect interests, majors, and careers.

Do *your* thing . . .

. . . not your parents'. If your parents want you to be a biologist and you're an artist, you'll never stay awake studying. It's too hard to get decent grades if you don't like your major.

Junior, Sociology, University of Colorado

The money motive. Don't make choosing your major a "career move." Pick what you really enjoy. Chances are the money will follow. If it doesn't, at least you'll like your job.

Graduate, Economics, Carleton College

The tunnel-vision trap. I just picked a major and stuck to the requirements so I'd be sure to graduate in four years. I keep thinking there were other majors I'd have enjoyed more . . ..

Senior, Political Science, University of California, Santa Cruz

Get real . . .

Until the day he flunked out, my roommate insisted that he was an "engineering major"—completely ignoring the fact that he was pretty bad in math and science. If he'd been realistic about his major, he'd still be here.

Senior, Accounting, Indiana University

Go with your natural ability. It probably isn't in a major where you have to kill yourself to get good grades.

Graduate, Marketing, University of Wisconsin

"Extraordinary drive comes from doing what you enjoy."

Patrick Combs

Experience counts . . .

Internships should be mandatory. Mine helped me figure out that I hated accounting, and it also helped me get my first job. It's a good way to test the waters *and* build a résumé.

Graduate, Business, Albion College

I always wanted to be a nurse—I thought. It wasn't until I started working in the hospital, AFTER struggling through a year and a half of tough science courses, that I realized *I don't even like being around sick people!* A little volunteer work or summer job would have told me that a lot sooner.

Junior, Education, University of Michigan

> Forget Burger King . . . find a summer job or volunteer doing something related to a career you may be interested in. It'll help you decide whether you are.
>
> *Junior, Business, Marquette University*

I'd have given up on an engineering degree because of all the math if I hadn't had a summer job with an engineering firm. It made me realize that's the career I really want. Now I'm willing to do what it takes to get there—and that's math.

Sophomore, Engineering, Michigan State University

Bottom Line: A JOB

Unless you're in engineering or accounting, or something specific like that, majors are pretty much interchangeable when it comes to getting a job. Eight of us were recently hired in this company, all with different majors.

Graduate, English, Indiana University

I don't even know what kind of job to look for, let alone where to find it. I wish I'd majored in something that directed me to a specific career—teaching, dietetics, accounting, something like that.

Senior, Humanities, Michigan State University

. . . one year later.

I landed a great job that has absolutely nothing to do with my major. I got it because of my work experience, campus activities, and good recommendations from both.

Graduate, Humanities, Michigan State University

My advice is _DON'T_ wait until your senior year to find out what the job prospects are in your major. If it's highly competitive, there are things you _need_ to do along the way to make yourself more marketable—pick up a minor, learn a language, volunteer . . . whatever.

Senior, Economics, University of Connecticut

Find out which majors at your school are considered "tops" in their field. You _might_ run across one you'd really like . . . and graduates from those majors are usually heavily recruited.

Graduate, Packaging, Michigan State University

Major in something you enjoy as an undergraduate and make it marketable in grad school.

Graduate, Education, Columbia University

The big picture . . .

I stuck with a major I wasn't crazy about because by the time I figured that out, I just wanted to finish school. It would have been smarter to have taken an extra year in college and ended up where I wanted to be. What's a year out of the rest of your life?

Graduate, Biology, University of Michigan

You can be totally immobilized if you think of choosing a major as what you're going to do with **"the rest of your life!?!"** For most people, it isn't. Looking back, I think it makes sense to choose a major based on what you enjoy. You're more likely to be enthusiastic and that's what opens doors. Besides, most entry-level jobs require skills you'll learn in ANY major.

Graduate, Education, University of Tennessee

When you first start college, you don't even know what questions to ask because you don't know what you should know . . ..

Senior, Education, St. Mary's College

Surviving 'The System'

F R O M   T H E   A D V I S O R

F R O M   T H E   A D V I S O R

That's a Good Question . . . Ask It!

What's the last day to add or drop a class—with and without the 100% refund? Is a drop noted on the transcript?

What are the minimum number of credits allowed to maintain eligibility for financial aid, scholarships, academic honors, health insurance, or living in the dorm?

What are the deadlines for application to various majors?

Is a "repeat" averaged with the original grade or does it replace it? How many repeats are allowed?

Can courses be taken for credit only, no grade, otherwise known as pass/fail? Will all majors accept them?

Who has the answers . . .?

Be kind to secretaries. They can make your life a lot easier and usually know more about the rules and regulations than instructors.

Senior, Film, San Francisco City College

There are advisers and there are *advisers*. The best thing I did was find one who was willing to do more than just okay my schedule.

Senior, Economics, University of Florida

I always started with the R.A. If she couldn't answer a question, she knew who could.

Senior, Economics, Carleton College

***Everything's* in the catalog** and that's the problem. Use the index.

Junior, Microbiology, Michigan State University

Get It In Writing!!!

Universities are notorious for screwing up. Keep all your receipts, copies of drops, adds, *anything that you had to get official permission to do.*

Senior, English, Rutgers University

Someone I saw my freshman year told me—or I thought she did—that I could substitute one of my requirements with another course. By my senior year, whoever it was, was gone and **there was nothing noted in my file.** I had to take the course.

Senior, Marketing, Ohio University

If you're sick, don't just lie around your room until you're better. Notify the instructor and see a doctor at the health center to get medicine *AND* verification. Profs are leery of scams.

Senior, Business, University of Toledo

Pre-register!!! Grab what classes you can even if you're unsure. You can drop and add later.

Junior, Geology, Arizona State University

If you want good advice, don't wait until the last minute to see advisers or professors. They'll be too busy to see you or too rushed to help you beyond the bare minimum. On a slow day they'll give you all kinds of help.

Senior, Political Science, Western Michigan University

Transfer tips, tricks . . .

Don't hesitate to transfer if you can't get into the program you want. I knew I wanted to be a teacher, so when I wasn't accepted, I transferred. In the long run, no one cares *where* your degree's from.
Eastern Michigan University

Credits transfer, grades don't—which makes junior colleges a good place to take tough courses without destroying a GPA. Classes are smaller too, so you're likely to get more attention.
University of Florida

Keep in touch with advisers at the school you want to transfer to. They'll tell you exactly which courses you should be taking and they'll know you're serious about transferring.
El Camino Junior College

When you're "explaining" a course you've taken somewhere else to the person deciding whether to accept that credit, make sure you *know the description of the "equivalent" course* at that school. A few well-chosen words or phrases can make all the difference.
Ohio University

. . . and traps.

Be prepared to hit the ground running when you transfer as a junior. You'll only have four semesters to establish your GPA. and it will be based on all upper level courses.

University of Colorado

Beware of "equivalents." No way did the course I took at another college during the summer prepare me for the follow-up course at my own school. It's better to take the *last* course in a sequence at another college, *not the first.*

University of Michigan

I felt like a "freshman" with junior status when I transferred . . . I was lost. Believe me, you're pretty much on your own—there's no big orientation. Get involved in activities and make a point of connecting with faculty as soon as possible.

Michigan State University

Do it *before* you're a junior if you plan to take a course at a community college. Credits from a two-year school may not be accepted after that.

Michigan State University

Note: Transfer rules vary from college to college. Check yours.

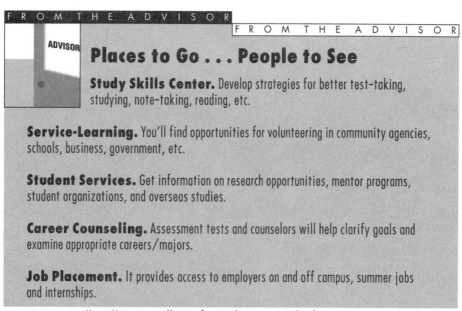

F R O M   T H E   A D V I S O R

ADVISOR

Places to Go . . . People to See

Study Skills Center. Develop strategies for better test-taking, studying, note-taking, reading, etc.

Service-Learning. You'll find opportunities for volunteering in community agencies, schools, business, government, etc.

Student Services. Get information on research opportunities, mentor programs, student organizations, and overseas studies.

Career Counseling. Assessment tests and counselors will help clarify goals and examine appropriate careers/majors.

Job Placement. It provides access to employers on and off campus, summer jobs and internships.

Note: Not every college refers to these services by the same name.

It's amazing how many things on this campus would really have been helpful if I'd known about them as a freshman instead of as a senior. **Nobody lays it out for you** . . . you have to find things yourself.

Senior, Environmental Science, University of Michigan

"About student loans . . . borrow only what you *need.* I always took the "max" since there were a lot of things I *needed*—a $1,000 mountain bike, a sound system, roller blades—I'll be paying for them until the year 2015."

Senior, Film, San Francisco City College

MONEY $$$

I visited the financial aid office during the summer before my freshman year. Classes hadn't started so they weren't swamped yet. **It was the best thing I ever did.** The adviser took a lot of time with me and got to know my situation. From then on, I always requested him. Over the course of my college career, he saw to it that I got some serious cash.

Graduate, Biology, University of Michigan

Double check your parent's work when it comes to the financial aid applications. An error can mean *major* delays.

Graduate, Education, Columbia University

I'm so mad at myself for not applying for any of the scholarships that were available. I didn't get one coming out of high school so I never gave it a second thought in college . . . **dumb!**

Senior, Human Communications, University of Connecticut

Note: There are private grants and scholarships available to existing students, often within the major. Check with your adviser.

BANKING AND CHECKING . . .

"Find a local bank or credit union and get your checking account going early. Almost no place accepts blank "starter" checks—you'll be out of luck for like 30 days."

"Choose a bank with a convenient ATM. If yours isn't, you'll end up using another and paying two bucks every time you need ten."

"No matter what, *DON'T* write your access code down on paper and send a friend to do your banking. *Borrow* money until you can do it yourself."

"Debit cards are easy. You don't have to carry much cash or write as many checks—*BUT you'd better know your balance!"*

Checking accounts teach you very quickly about "high finance." After being charged \$27.50 a few times for overdrawing, I learned.

Sophomore, Engineering, Notre Dame

Note: Get overdraft protection. It's worth it—as long as you don't use it as credit. The interest can bury you.

CREDIT CARDS . . .

"Use 'plastic' to pay tuition. The Frequent Flier points are *huge,* which means free air fare to and from school—or *maybe* Cancun?"

"Never get a cash advance on a credit card. The interest accumulates *daily* and will kill you."

"IF you pay on time, a credit card is a good way to establish credit. Otherwise, it's a good way to destroy it."

"Paying *only* the minimum balance is a sure way to Credit Card Hell."

"There's a 24-hour phone number on the back of your card. Keep it somewhere handy so you can report a lost card *immediately.*"

Every college student should have a credit card, even if it's just for emergencies. *But* make sure you're clear on the definition of "emergency." For me it was every time I went into The GAP—**until my dad saw the bill.**

Sophomore, History, University of Pennsylvania

THE PHONE BILL . . .

"Don't call collect and especially don't bill to a third number. It's astronomical."

"Don't put the phone in your name if you can avoid it. It's a pain to divvy up the charges among roommates and a bigger pain to collect."

"Use e-mail and have your parents get an 800 number."

"My parents pay for a phone card so I can call home, and I have my own card for calling friends. Everybody's happy."

Cars on CAMPUS

Parking on campus is a nightmare. Out of *desperation* you always end up parking in restricted areas. I had to take out a short-term note just to pay off parking tickets and tow charges before I was allowed to register.

Senior, Telecommunications, Michigan State University

Note: Parents, you may be able to get lower auto insurance rates if your student is more than 100 miles from home and doesn't have a car at school.

A JOB⁉⁉⁉

Don't get a job until after your freshman
year . . . or whenever you've figured out how
to manage your time.

Senior, Economics, University of Florida

It's a trade-off. I was working so many hours that I had to cut back on credits. In the long run, it's cost me. I'm taking longer to graduate and it'll be that much longer before I'm making *real* money.

Junior, Business, University of Alabama

If there's nothing much to do, I don't do much of anything, including study. I manage my time better when I'm working 15 to 20 hours a week.

Senior, Business, University of Toledo

A job gets you 'out there' —you meet more people and connect on different levels. Even if it's only a few hours, it's *important* to work ...or volunteer or *do something*.

Junior, Psychology, Colgate University

A good piece of work . . .

Get a job in the office of your major. You'll get to know everyone from the secretaries to the dean, all of whom can be very helpful. If any great opportunities come along, you'll be the first to know.

Senior, Environmental Science, Indiana University

QUICK TIPS

"The good jobs go fast. Start looking early."

"Work your tail off in the summer so you don't have to work during the school year."

"Find a job in something related to your major."

"Don't work in restaurants unless you wait tables. That's where the money is."

"Find a job where you can study."

"*DO NOT* work more than 20 hours a week if you're carrying a full load."

> **"Kids bring all 500 CD's and they're left with 200 at the end of the first week. It leaves them scarred for the rest of college."**
>
> Senior, Accounting, Indiana University

Crime Stoppers

Outta sight . . .

People are always in and out of the room watching movies, using the computer or just hanging out. Anything I care about, I keep out of sight.

Sophomore, Business, University of Alabama

Don't leave your valuables in the car, or at least not where they're visible. My books and golf clubs were stolen. The books didn't bother me . . ..

Senior, Communications, University of Toledo

Label everything . . .

It's just like going to camp—put your name on everything! There's a guy walking around campus in what I *know* is *my* $200 jacket, but I've got no proof. I'm *ticked* every time I see him!

Senior, Marketing, Ohio University

Your stuff's fair game if you leave it in someone else's room. My Providence Friars hat had a whole life of its own. Every time I saw it on campus, a different kid was wearing it.

Junior, Kinesiology, University of Michigan

Leave the good stuff at home . . .

Don't bring an expensive bike. Even with the best lock it'll get ripped off piecemeal . . . or rust.

Ohio State University

The Gucci watch you got for graduation is as good as gone in the dorm. Bring a Timex.

Indiana University

Don't prop doors. Even if *you* don't care about your worldly possessions, your roommate or suitemates will.

University of Rhode Island

Note: Your parent's homeowner's insurance may extend to your personal property while living in the dorm.

Keep your eyes on the prize . . .

Some people shop in the laundry more often than the mall. Don't leave clothes in the washer or dryer and expect them to be there when you return!

Senior, Accounting, University of Michigan

When you're in the shower, make sure you can see your towel and clothes at all times. It's a long walk back to your room without them.

Sophomore, Premed, Cornell University

Watch your computer access number. Someone can mess around with your schedule or drop your classes and you have no way to prove it wasn't you that did it.

Senior, Packaging, Michigan State University

Avoiding creeps, perverts, & lowlifes

Know the campus bus schedule and plan on leaving before the last run of the night. *Michigan State University*

Stick to public places when you go out with someone you don't know well. *University of Iowa*

Friends take care of friends. You can do some dumb things when you're partying. Go in groups. *M.I.T.*

Keep your finger on the button. Mace or pepper spray won't do any good in your purse. *Columbia University*

Let people know where you're going and when you'll be back. If your plans change, call. *Butler University*

Don't go *near* a bedroom if you're high. *Rollins College*

Dating DILEMMAS

If a girl even hints at "no" or "stop," pay attention. My friend was accused of rape, and even though the charges were eventually dropped, it was devastating to his family and he was dropped from the fraternity he was pledging.

Senior, Accounting, University of Michigan

Note: The highest incidence of sexual assault is among freshmen and is most likely to occur during the first 3 months on campus.

"You could party every night of the week if you wanted to. *Pace yourself!!!* You have to know *when* to have fun and *when* to get serious!

Junior, Geology, Arizona State University

Partying & Stuff

PARTYING & STUFF

For the Record

Really, you don't *have* to drink. The only time people think you're weird is when you sit around doing nothing. Just *go* to the parties. No one notices *what* you do once you're there.

University of California/Santa Cruz

Baby-sitting friends who are habitually tanked gets real old, real fast.

University of Wyoming

In college it's easy to do your own thing. If you don't drink, it's not a big deal.

Macalester College

Some schools can be anal about the rules on alcohol in the dorms. Be sure you know the consequences. Around here you'll get busted big time.

University of Arizona

You can always tell freshmen. They act like they've just been let off the leash.

Senior, Business, Northern Illinois University

It's hard to believe what a straight-arrow I was in high school . . . National Honor Society and the whole thing. I've basically screwed myself so far in college. My entire freshman year "went up in smoke," if you know what I mean. I barely even remember the names of my courses, let alone going to them. **I guess the party's over**—along with my scholarship.

If you pour it . . . they will come

Keg parties can get huge and out of control instantly. They're great to go to, but unless you're living in a dump, I wouldn't throw one.

Junior, Business, Miami of Ohio

Drinking games get you wrecked in a hurry. There's nothing wrong with substituting a Coke—if you can take a little ragging. Actually, there's nothing wrong with watching, either. It's usually more laughs.

Junior, Education, Central Michigan University

If you're offered a "Bud," it isn't beer. Nobody cares whether you take it or leave it. It's not like you're going to impress someone . . . The only pressure is from yourself.

Junior, Sociology, University of Colorado

The Bar Buzz

"'B' is for 'buzz,' not 'binge,' not 'bombed'. Stay lucid."

"Stick to the buddy system. Don't go to parties alone and *definitely* don't walk home from parties alone—that means guys too. A friend of mine was beaten bloody just for sport."

"Pool your money for a cab. It's a good time and nobody ends up with a *DWI—or worse*."

"Fake I.D. might get you in . . . or 100 hours of community service and a $500 fine."

"Wear 'designated party shoes.' They get destroyed in crowds."

Know when to fold 'em . . .

Sports gambling is huge in the dorms and easy to get hooked on since it makes watching games with a bunch of guys really exciting. A friend of mine had to sell his Jeep to cover his losses . . . and *that* was calling "lock lines" which are supposed to be *sure* things.

Junior, Criminal Justice, Saint Joseph's University

I was losing twenty bucks a night just playing cards on our floor! It's easy to get sucked into that stuff when there's a bunch of guys around and you don't feel like studying.

Graduate, Business, Albion College

College towns are exciting. You meet people from different backgrounds with different values. Know what yours are and stick to them.

Junior, Economics, Duke University

"I wouldn't want to pay money to have friends . . .
but fraternity guys *do* meet a lot of girls."

Senior, Economics, University of Florida

To be or not to be . . .
GREEK

Greek musings . . .

At some schools you're either Greek, an athlete, or you sit around doing nothing on weekends. *Miami of Ohio*

It's a good way to make a big school feel small. Classes at most universities are huge and you really don't get to know anyone. Sororities make it easier, less isolating. *University of Iowa*

I'd miss a lot if I were wrapped up in a sorority. I'd rather be involved in campus sports, clubs, plays, and things like that. *M.I.T.*

Fraternities make it easy to socialize when you don't have a lot of time. There's always a party or something going on. *Colgate University*

I've never worked so hard in my life. We were forever fundraising or doing some charity thing and someone was always griping about how it *should* have been done. *Michigan State University*

It's a great network during and after college. I have fraternity brothers all over the country. Someone's always got a father or an uncle who can open a door for you. *Colgate University*

I don't think it's worth it. If you're worried about networking and resumes, get out in the community and meet people, get involved in a research project. That's likely to be more helpful in the long run. *Aquinas College*

Sometimes it gets to be too much. You're always worried about your "image." Someone always wants to know, "Who did you go out with?" "What did you wear?" "Who was there?" "Why aren't you doing this or that?" *Indiana University*

Greeks always know what's happening on campus, which courses are good, who's the best prof, job openings, parties. All that, *plus* test files! *Ohio State University*

What's the "Rush?"

I rushed the first house I walked into my first semester and spent a lot of time washing dishes and scrubbing floors before I figured out that it wasn't the place for me. Don't rush your first semester. Get to *know* guys from different fraternities and what's going on in them.

Senior, Accounting, Indiana University

Forget which house is "cool" or who has the best "national." Look for people you're comfortable with. If you have to act like something you're not just to fit in, it's not worth it.

Sophomore, Premed, Cornell University

I dropped out of rush when my roommate didn't get a bid. Shortly thereafter, she ended up pregnant and left school. I ended up wishing I was in a sorority. You need to do what's best for *you*.

Junior, Psychology, Southern Illinois University

Pledging is like taking an additional four credits, at least. Plan your schedule accordingly.

Senior, Economics, University of Connecticut

Some fraternities make it impossible to get decent grades while you're pledging. **My G.P.A. never recovered.** If grades are your priority, make sure there's at least *some* value placed on academics in the house you're pledging.

Senior, Business, Northern Illinois University

BEWARE of Greeks

Greek at one school can be totally different from Greek at another. Ours is big on parties, but sports, academics, and community service are big too. At my brother's school, **the houses are trashed and so are the guys** most of the time. Their idea of sports is playing SEGA while smoking a joint.

Senior, Marketing, Ohio University

The biggest use of drugs and alcohol is in the fraternities.

Junior, Geology, Arizona State University

Everyone hazes. It ranges from mild harassment to perverted and dangerous. Unfortunately you never know which until you're in the middle of it. By then, not only have you invested a huge amount of time, but you also don't want to look like a wimp by bailing out.

Sophomore, Advertising, University of Florida

After making it through a whole semester of pledging, our "I" Week, otherwise known as **"HELL WEEK,"** turned out to be two weeks—one for the official initiation and another for the "unofficial" one. The fact that no one was allowed to study during either, forced two of us to decide whether we wanted to be Sigma Chi's or M.D.'s . . . .

Junior, Biology, University of Michigan

" College was what I wanted to do socially, not academically. I wish I'd taken it more seriously. "

Graduate, English, Rutgers University

Ah Ha!

Words from the wise . . .

Going to college was for my parents. It wasn't until I realized I was there for myself that I got serious. Unfortunately, that was pretty late in the game. Somehow it has to become *your* goal . . . the sooner, the better.

Graduate, Logistics Management, Michigan State University

I wish I hadn't put so much pressure on myself. There were so many things going on that I missed. I should have relaxed and enjoyed it more . . . done things because I wanted to, not because it looked good on a résumé.

Graduate, English, Indiana University

College was just the next thing to do...and I could play soccer. At some point, it occurred to me that I really LIKED to learn and LIKED to talk to people about what they'd learned. I never knew that . . ..

Senior, Sociology, University of Colorado

Geez, where do I start . . .? There are *so many* things I wish I'd done . . . I could kick myself for not realizing that college was probably the *only* time I'd have the freedom *and* the opportunity to explore options and try a lot of different things. After you graduate, it's all about paying bills . . . there's no time and no opportunity for much else.

Graduate, Marketing, University of Wisconsin

WHAT IT'S ALL ABOUT . . .

You don't "get it" when you're in college. It's not about what you major in or which classes you take . . . you won't remember most of them anyway. It's really about learning to *think* and to *communicate. Wherever* you end up, you'll need to be able to analyze and solve problems—to figure out what needs to be done and do it! "Doing it" takes being organized, having the ability to express yourself effectively, and a lot of other skills you didn't realize you were learning in some of those "boring, senseless" courses. You can definitely scam your way through college without developing those skills . . . a lot of kids do . . . but in the long run, **you're only limiting yourself.** Trust me, that can make your first job a little scary.

Graduate, Marketing, Ohio University

I have like thirty days until I graduate and I'm so depressed . . . It took me until my senior year to appreciate the fact that I can walk right out my door and learn anything I want . . . **it's all right here.** College puts you in touch with so much . . . so many kinds of people, so many opportunities to try things. I'm more accepting, more open . . .. It takes every college student a while to figure things out, but I'd definitely say, "Take advantage of the fact that you're there. Enjoy."

Senior, Human Development, University of Connecticut

Thanks to the experts . . .

(Contributions were made by students from the following colleges.)

Adelphi University
University of Alabama
Albion College
Alma College
Arizona State University
Aquinas College
Bowling Green State University
Butler University
UCLA
University of California,
  Santa Cruz
Carleton College
Central Michigan University

Colgate University
University of Colorado
Columbia University
University of Connecticut
Cornell University
Denison University
DePaul University
Duke University
Eastern Michigan University
El Camino Junior College
Ferris State University
University of Florida
Grand Valley State University

Hope College
Indiana University
University of Iowa
Kalamazoo College
Lansing Community College
Macalester College
Marquette University
Miami University
Michigan State University
University of Michigan
M.I.T.
Northern Illinois University
Northwestern College
Notre Dame
Ohio State University
Ohio University

University of Pennsylvania
University of Rhode Island
Rollins College
Rutgers University
Saint Joseph's University
St. Mary's College
San Francisco City College
Southern Illinois University
University of Tennessee
University of Toledo
Valparaiso University
Vanderbilt University
Western Michigan University
Williams College
University of Wisconsin
University of Wyoming

"#*@!!!, where was this book when I needed it?!?"

SHARE YOUR TIPS

There's nothing better than the voice of experience. If you have any "hot tips" or words of wisdom you'd like to share, please do at

styler@voyager.net
FAX: (517) 487-0888

Front Porch Press
P.O. Box 234
Haslett, MI 48840